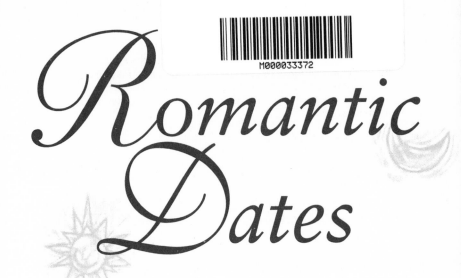

Romantic Dates

Gregory J.P. Godek

bestselling author of *1001 Ways to Be Romantic*

CASABLANCA PRESS
A DIVISION OF SOURCEBOOKS
NAPERVILLE, IL

Published by: Sourcebooks, Inc.
P.O. Box 372, Naperville, Illinois 60566
(630) 961-3900
FAX: (630) 961-2168

Cover design by Scott Theisen
Internal design and production by Andrew Sardina, Scott Theisen and Joe Leamon

$\mathcal{D}$edication

To those who see dating as a way of relating,
and not merely impressing.

And, of course, to my Bride—my date, my mate.

Library of Congress Cataloging-in-Publication Data
Godek, Gregory J.P.
        Romantic Dates : ways to woo & wow the ones you love / Gregory
    J.P. Godek.
                p.   cm. -- (A Casablanca book)
        ISBN 1-57071-153-4 (pap)
        1. Dating (Social customs) 2. Courtship. 3. Man-woman
relationships. 4. Love.   I. Title.
HQ801.G565 1997
306.73--dc21   96-52863
                                                                    CIP

Printed and bound in the United States of America.

10 9 8 7 6 5 4 3 2 1

Contents

Introduction

$\mathcal{D}$ating should be taught in school, don't you think? Not only are dating skills more important than algebra, they will serve you throughout your life l-o-o-o-n-g after quadratic equations cease having the slightest relevance to your existence.

But since dating isn't taught in school, we'll just have to teach ourselves, won't we? In my 17 years of presenting Romance Classes, researching love and interviewing couples, I've learned that love must be lived and expressed if it is to stay alive. I've also learned that dating is one of the best— and simplest—ways of keeping love alive.

Whether you're single or married, successful dating is about expressing love, expressing yourself and getting to know your partner. It's about doing things together, creating shared memories and acknowledging one another. This book is a collection of old and new ideas—from the *1001 Ways to Be Romantic* series of books, from my seminars, and from my readers—all designed to turn you into a dating dynamo.

My hope is that you become inspired to keep dating throughout your life, and that you become the inspiration for younger couples looking for romantic role models.

Gregory J.P. Godek
January 1997

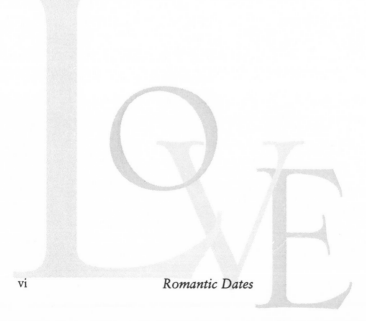

Romantic Dates

Romantic Days

1
. . .

*O*ne day in the Romance Class, Nancy G. told us that she and her husband have instituted a "Play Day" once a month. The class quickly leaped on the idea and expanded upon it. So we now have couples celebrating their own "Music Days," "Food Days," and—of course—"Sex Days."

2
. . .

*Y*ou could create special "themes" for various days.

- ✾ A "food" theme: Focus your entire day around food. Prepare a special breakfast. Go shopping at a farmers' market. Plan many tasty surprises for your partner throughout the day.

- ✾ A "sensual" theme: Focus your entire day around your five senses. Create experiences that heighten your appreciation of the sensual aspects of life.

Give each other body massages. Watch the sunrise. Bake bread so you can appreciate the aroma. Attend a concert to appreciate the sounds.

∽ A "sexual" theme: Focus your entire day around the expression and celebration of your sexual natures. Touch each other often, from the moment you wake up in the morning. Dress provocatively. Make love several times, in several locations, throughout the day. Rent some erotic movies. Act out a favorite fantasy.

3

*W*eekdays are for working, and weekends are for relaxing. Sez who?? Even though Saturdays and Sundays are great days for romance, so are Monday, Tuesday, Wednesday, Thursday and Friday!

While "Weekend Romance" can be leisurely and event-filled, "Weekday Romance" can be spontaneous, quick and fun! Think about it.

Romantic Nights

1
. . .

$\mathscr{D}$inner by candlelight. The classics always work (as long as you get the kids out of the picture and unplug the phone).

2
. . .

$\mathscr{O}$n your way home from work, pick up a bottle of champagne and one red rose. (The classics always work!)

3
. .

$\mathscr{T}$ake all the furniture out of your dining room. Roll up the rug. Move your stereo speakers into the room. Dig-out your favorite dance tunes. Greet him or her at the door dressed in your finest…and dance the night away!

Cheap Dates

1

*N*ote: There's a significant difference between being a cheap date and going on a cheap date!

2

*M*ovie matinees. Cheap but still fun.

3

*G*o shopping at second-hand shops and vintage clothing stores. It might spark some fun dress-up fantasies!

4

*Y*our basic wine and cheese picnic.

Inspired Dates

1

$\mathcal{W}$hat's more inspiring than a magnificent sunrise—or a spectacular sunset? Pack a breakfast, head for a quiet spot and enjoy the sunrise together. Or make time for a sunset dinner.

2

$\mathcal{T}$ake a seminar together: A Dale Carnegie class or Tony Robbins seminar will inspire you and help your relationship in many ways!

3

$\mathcal{G}$rab some crayons or markers, title two sheets of poster paper "100 Reasons Why I Love You," and spend an evening (or two) expressing your appreciation for your mate.

Classic Dates

1

$\mathcal{D}$inner and a movie. Note: See the movie first. That way you won't have to rush through dinner. Plus, you can discuss the movie afterward over a leisurely meal.

2

$\mathcal{D}$inner and dancing. (And if you don't know how to dance, sign-up for some dance classes! Between the lessons and your own practice sessions you'll be busy for months!)

3

$\mathcal{A}$ bicycle built for two.

4

A walk on the beach.

5

A stroll in the park.

6

The scene: a pond. The equipment: a canoe. The food: picnic style. The characters: the two of you.

Classy Dates

1

Hire a pianist to come to your home and provide live background music to a private romantic dinner.

2

$\mathcal{H}$ire a limousine for the evening. Dress up and go out. But don't stop anywhere—just drive around for few hours...sipping champagne and seeing the sights.

3

$\mathcal{T}$ake a wine tasting course together. Then attend wine tastings at various wine shops around town. This little hobby will keep you occupied and fascinated for years to come.

4

$\mathcal{T}$our a winery. Tour wineries in all 41 states that produce wine!

Strategies for Creating Romantic Dates

1
. . .

$\mathscr{Y}$ou say you just don't have time for romantic dates? The #1 time-stealer is television. Try this experiment: Stop watching TV for one solid month. I'll bet your time shortage will evaporate.

2
. . .

$\mathscr{R}$ight-brained vs. left-brained romance. Which is your style? Right-brainers are emotional, creative and intuitive. Left-brainers are logical, detail-oriented and organized.

❧ Right-brainers tend to be good at creating experiences, moods and memories. They'll head for a movie on a whim; cook a romantic meal from leftovers; write three love notes while their partner is looking the other way.

Ways to Woo and Wow the One You Love   9

- Left-brainers tend to be good at planning, scheduling and organizing. They'll create great surprise parties; never forget an anniversary; buy gifts ahead of time.

Personal Holidays

1
· · ·

*L*et's face it: Valentine's Day puts too much pressure on all of us. This one day is going to make up for all the other days we act like romantic blockheads?! I think not. The solution? Create your own romantic holidays!

- Celebrate Valentine's Day on the 14th day of every month, all year round!

- Create your own "Lovers' Day" in April, July and November.

- Create a floating holiday: Set-aside one Friday every other month; take the day off work; create a three-day escape weekend.

2
. . .

*H*ow about creating special "Half-Day Holidays"—for those of you who would have a hard time taking off a whole day of work?

3
. . .

*T*here are all kinds of crazy, special and unique reasons to celebrate, and most of them are listed in a cool book called *Celebrate Today*, by John Kremer.

Making Beautiful Music Together

1
. . .

*C*reate a Valentine's Day concert, just for the two of you. Record an hour's worth of your favorite romantic music. Print-up a program. List the song titles, along with some personal commentary about the significance of each song to you, or why particular songs remind you of her. Send her an invitation to the concert. Dress for the event. Serve wine and cheese.

2

*C*urrent romantic favorites in the Godek Music Library:

- *Shepherd Moons*, by Enya
- *In the Garden*, by Eric Tingstad & Nancy Rumbel
- *Reference Point*, by Acoustic Alchemy

3

*L*earn to sing your favorite love song together—in harmony!

4

$\mathscr{L}$earn to sing a romantic duet! Some suggestions:

- *Almost Paradise*, by Reno & Wilson
- *Nothing's Gonna Stop Us Now*, by Starship
- *Always*, by Atlantic Starr
- *Islands in the Stream*, by Parton & Rogers
- *Somewhere Out There*, by Ronstadt & Ingram
- *Time of My Life*, by Medley & Warnes

5

$\mathscr{T}$ake each other somewhere special:

- Has she seen all of her favorite singers in concert?
- Has he heard all of his favorite symphonies played live?
- Has she traveled to her dream vacation spot?
- Has he seen his favorite team play live?

Romantic Travel

1

$\mathcal{A}$ vacation is just a vacation—but you can turn it into a honeymoon by adding romantic elements. And *Honeymoon* Magazine combines those elements. NOT for newlyweds only!!

2

$\mathcal{S}$ome travel newsletters:

- ❧ Travel Smart—800-FARE-OFF
- ❧ The Educated Traveler—703-471-1063

3

$\mathcal{W}$hile on vacation some couples spend as little as possible on accommodations and as much as possible on dining out!

Other couples pamper themselves with the most luxurious room they can find, and cut corners on meals.

Some couples cut back on room and board so they can spend their money on mementos of their travels.

Travel Tips

1

$\mathcal{D}$oes she love ice cream as much as she loves you? Take her on a tour of Ben & Jerry's factory in Waterbury, Vermont! Call 802-244-TOUR.

2

$\mathcal{D}$oes he crave beer as much as he craves you? Take him to the world's largest brewery, Anheuser-Busch, in St. Louis, Missouri. Call 314-577-2626.

3
. . .

$\mathcal{I}$s she a certified chocoholic? Take her to
Hershey's Chocolate World, in Hershey,
Pennsylvania. Call 717-534-4900.

A Week of Romance

1
. . .

$\mathcal{S}$unday—Read the Sunday newspapers in bed. Or
go out for Sunday brunch.

2
. . .

$\mathcal{M}$onday—You could make Mondays much
more manageable if...you get up an hour early,
serve breakfast in bed and enjoy one another's
company—before facing the world.

3
···

*T*uesday—Get the Moody Blues' CD *Days of Future Passed*. Play the song "Tuesday Afternoon." Then, schedule-in a little afternoon delight with your honey.

4
···

*W*ednesday—Commonly known as "Hump Day" because it's in the middle of the week…could be interpreted in another fashion, too!

5
···

*T*hursday—Pick-up some videos for the weekend—beat the weekend crowds.

6
···

*F*riday—TGIF! Call-in sick to work.

7
···

*S*aturday—Sleep-in late. Weekend getaways. Saturday Night at the Movies.

Good Times

1

A day at the beach.
A night at the opera.

2

A walk in the park.
A stroll down memory lane.

3

A midnight snack.
*A*n afternoon tea.

4

A drive in the country.
A tour of the city.

Movie Dates

1

Favorite romantic movies (current):

- *When Harry Met Sally*
- *Bull Durham*
- *Flashdance*
- *Ghost*
- *Gone with the Wind*
- *A Place in the Sun*
- *Suddenly Last Summer*
- *Raintree County*
- *Splendor in the Grass*
- *Brief Encounter*
- *Frankie and Johnny*

2

. . .

*F*avorite romantic movies (classic):

- *A Woman of Affairs*
- *Hold Your Man*
- *Saratoga*
- *Blossoms in the Dust*
- *Maytime*
- *Strike Up the Band*
- *Double Wedding*
- *Top Hat*
- *Carefree*
- *From the Terrace*
- *The Big Sleep*
- *Key Largo*

3

Create a "movie weekend" based on a theme:

- All adventure movies, romantic movies or science fiction movies
- Movies starring her favorite actor
- Movies starring his favorite actress
- All Academy Award winning movies
- Foreign films
- All movies by a favorite writer or director

Fantasy Dates

1

"Donald Trump Day": Pretend you're millionaires. Test drive a Porsche. Window shop at Tiffany's. Try on fur coats. Visit mansions for sale.

2

"*B*onnie and Clyde Day": Be wild! I don't recommend that you actually rob a bank—but you could certainly withdraw money from an ATM machine and pretend! (I don't think there's anything illegal about wearing a mask into a bank!)

3

"*P*eter Pan Day": Refuse to grow up! Play hookey from work. Go to a carnival. Be silly. Buy a balloon. Play a board game.

Erotica

1

*I*f your life was a movie…and you were going to film a scene in which you seduce your partner… and you want this scene to be elegant and romantic…how would you create this scene? What would the dialogue be? What gifts/props would you use? What would the lighting be?

2
. . .

S.O.S.—"Sex On Saturday"! Leave this "distress" message on her answering machine; mark it in his calendar; mail her S.O.S. notes; create a banner; make a "doorknob sign."

3
. . .

Some books on erotica and sex—sure to inspire some sexy dates:

- *It Is Indiscreet*, by David Loth
- *Women Who Love Sex*, by Gina Ogden
- *203 Ways to Drive a Man Wild in Bed*, by Olivia St. Claire

Romantic Planning

1
. . .

A romantic's planning calendar:

*J*anuary: Sit with your partner and review the upcoming year. Make reservations at a bed & breakfast for Valentine's Day.

*F*ebruary: Plan your summer vacation and any other major vacations. Plan a "Springtime Get-Away" as a surprise.

*M*arch: Begin your Christmas shopping.

*A*pril: Call local theatres, symphonies and ticket agencies to get their upcoming schedules. Order tickets well in advance.

*M*ay: Make your plans for summer.

*J*une: Schedule-in a three-day escape for some-time between Memorial Day and Labor Day.

*A*ugust: Plan a leaf-peeping excursion.

October: Plan a ski weekend for the upcoming winter.

November: Buy greeting cards for every occasion you can think of. Spend at least $200.

December: Look at a calendar for next year. Brainstorm twelve new romantic ideas.

A Year of Romance

1
. . .

For each month of the year, define a "theme" or "topic" to focus on as a couple. For example:

January: Renewal
February: Playing
March: Sensuality
April: Communication
May: Learning

June: Intimacy

July: Commitment

August: Celebrating

September: Self-esteem

October: Change

November: Forgiveness

December: Appreciation

2

Spin-off ideas from the idea above:

- ❧ Define themes for each day of the week. You'll cycle through the list 52 times in a year, giving you variety and repetition.

- ❧ Define themes for your weekends.

- ❧ One couple in the Romance Class is compiling a list of 365 themes, one for each day of the week. (Some romantics are obsessed!)

Romantic Rituals

1

$\mathscr{D}$eclare your anniversary and both of your birthdays to be your own, special "Couple's Holidays." Take those days off work and get away by yourselves. Don't let jobs or kids get in your way!

2

$\mathscr{W}$hen you celebrate the "official" holidays of our culture, focus on the true and original meanings of the events, and don't let society's commercialism ruin it for you.

3

$\mathscr{C}$reate your own special "holidays." I know people who celebrate the first day of summer, autumn, winter and spring. Others celebrate the first day of school by staying home and making love in the family room! Some people celebrate the first snow fall of the year, or the first day of fishing season.

*C*reate your own unique rituals. (A ritual is a special activity you perform that highlights an occasion and gives it deeper meaning.) The occasion can be commonplace or rare.

Commonplace rituals could be:

- Always greeting one another with a slow kiss.

- Preparing for lovemaking in a special, meaningful manner.

- A call from work at the same time every day.

Rare rituals could be:

- A secret toast to one another while out to dinner with friends.

- A unique celebration of each other's career milestones.

- Time spent together before one of you leaves for a trip.

On August 3, 1964, during a walk on the beach with his wife, Howard W. drew a heart in the sand, and inscribed his initials entwined with his wife's initials. The next day when they returned to the same spot (near their home on Cape Cod, Massachusetts), the surf had washed his handiwork away. Undaunted, he drew the same message again, saying, "Love needs to be renewed every day, too." Howard has drawn the same heart and initials in the sand every day for the past 30 years!

Honeymoon Heaven

1
. . .

A plain old vacation is not the same thing as a "second honeymoon"! There's a special feeling of magic and romance around a second honeymoon.

How do you create one? You start planning about a year in advance (so the anticipation builds). You buy her a stack of brides magazines (that's where all the honeymoon destination ads are). Send travel brochures to her in the mail (with your personal notes and comments written-in). You buy special clothes.

If you do this right, it'll really spice up your life—for a year or more!

2
. . .

Go on a last-minute vacation. Don't even pack any clothes—buy them there!

3
. . .

Do you and your partner have the same "Vacation Style"? Are you an "Adventurer," "Sight-Seer," "Romantic," "Shopper," "Athlete," or "Indulger"? Do you choose vacation destinations and activities that match your styles? How do you compromise when you have different styles?

A Night on the Town

1

$\mathscr{F}$or some people, an evening out is about ambiance and relaxing. Dinner at a quiet, dim restaurant. Conversation at a scenic location. Taking in a local amateur theatre show.

2

$\mathscr{F}$or other people, an evening out is about adventure and excitement. Making the scene at the hottest nightclub. Dancing the night away. Visiting a new restaurant.

3

$\mathscr{H}$ave you ever tried "Restaurant-Hopping"? You spend the entire evening hopping from one restaurant to another, having only one course in each establishment:

- Drinks
- Appetizer

- Soup
- Salad
- Main course
- Dessert
- After-dinner drinks

For Marrieds Only

1

. . .

*H*ow many people do you know who've celebrated 288 anniversaries? Well, meet the Claytons, of Nebraska. "We've celebrated our wedding anniversary every month for 24 years now. We don't buy gifts every month (we'd be more broke than we are now!) but we do recognize it somehow: with a kiss, a flower, or a short note."

2

*P*lanning to renew your wedding vows in a second ceremony? (You romantic fools, you!) These books may help make the occasion extra special:

- *Weddings for Grownups*, by Carroll Stoner
- *I Do: A Guide to Creating Your Own Unique Wedding Ceremony*, by Sydney Barbara Metrick
- *Weddings By Design*, by Richard Leviton

3

*D*eclare it "Wife Appreciation Day"—and act accordingly.

4

*D*eclare him "Husband of the Year"—and treat him like a king for a day.

5

Many couples report fond memories of the time and place that they first met; some of them visit their meeting place yearly; and many of them make a pilgrimage on their 10th, 20th, 25th, 30th, or 40th anniversaries.

Pillowtalk

1

Your bed is a great place to have intimate conversations. Do you give yourselves enough time to lounge, laugh, love and talk in bed?

2

If you were going to spend an entire Sunday in bed with your lover, what supplies would you need in order to make your bedroom a self-sufficient oasis?

One Day at a Time

1

$\mathscr{G}$ive your partner a day. Devote a solid 24 hours to him or her. Take 24 slips of paper; number them 1 through 24, and write on each one: "What would you like to do at 6 a.m.?" "What would you like to do at 7 a.m.?" etc.

Wrap your stack of 24 hours in an elegant little gift box, along with a new pen (maybe a fancy fountain pen). Your partner will have fun deciding what to do during his or her day—and you'll both have fun living through that special day.

2

$\mathscr{F}$ind an "extra" day in the next month, and devote that day to your partner. Find or create that extra day by rearranging your schedule; being more efficient at work; delegating some of that work to someone else; limiting your social commitments; paying some neighbor kids to do your weekend chores.

Tickets

1

*A*lways have at least one set of tickets for an upcoming event tacked to your bulletin board. It's always good to have some special event to look forward to. (The anticipation is half the fun!)

2

"*C*hoice seats on short notice"—great tickets for Broadway shows, sports events and concerts. Call Tickets On Request at 212-967-5600.

3

*I*t's romantic—but not that unusual—to have tickets to the opera or the Red Sox. Some offbeat romantics have created their own custom "tickets" to the following events and activities:

- Dinner for two. (Reserved seating only.)
- Season tickets for "Friday Night Mattress Testing."

❧ A personal striptease. (Front row seat guaranteed.)

Outdoor Adventures

1
. . .

*C*amp-out in your backyard.

2
. . .

*P*lay miniature golf...while dressed in your wedding gown and tuxedo!

3
. . .

*Y*our basic picnic.

4
. . .

*O*n a summer day...Lie on your backs in a field... Look for shapes in the clouds...Hang out for a couple hours...Talk about your hopes and dreams.

5

*O*n a summer night…Within a night or two of August 12th every year you can see dozens of shooting stars every hour! The earth passes through the Perseid Meteor Belt at the same time each year, and we get treated to a show!

6

*G*o parking! (While not officially an "outdoor" activity, we'll let you get away with it.)

7

*G*o on an Outward Bound weekend (or vacation!). Guaranteed to change your perspective on life. Call 800-243-8520.

Festivals!

1

*S*treet fairs, county fairs, state fairs!

2

Carnivals and amusement parks!

3

Balloon festivals, food festivals, art festivals!

Dinner for Two

1

Try this next Saturday evening: Prepare a five-course dinner—and serve each course in a different room of your home. Choose any rooms you wish, but dessert must be served in the bedroom. Bon appétit!

2

Have a special dinner catered for the two of you at home. No muss, no fuss—just pay for it!

*C*reate a meal in which every item of food is fashioned into the shape of a heart.

At-Home Dates

1
· · ·

*H*old a conversation with your lover in the dark. Shut out inputs from your other senses, and focus on the sound of your partner's voice: its ups and downs, its unique qualities and quirks. Listen for the love behind the words. Listen. Listen. Listen!

2
· · ·

*P*erhaps a hammock would bring the two of you together. Swing lazily between two trees.

3
· · ·

*C*reate a "Five-Sense Evening," during which you

and your lover stimulate all five of each other's senses. Enjoy!

4
. . .

$\mathscr{D}$o you have a porch? Do you have a porch swing? What more could you ask for?

5
. . .

$\mathscr{TV}$ dates! If you limit yourself to one or two special shows per week, it can be special, instead of a mind-numbing, time consuming habit.

6
. . .

$\mathscr{W}$atch "Mad About You"—the most romantic show on TV.

7
. . .

$\mathscr{P}$lant a garden together. (This will provide you with many built-in dates all summer long.)

Learning & Loving

1

$\int$pend an afternoon teaching each other to do something you're good at, and that your partner wants to learn: cook a special meal; throw a frisbee; change a flat tire; sew a button; play a video game.

2

$\int$tart a collection together: stamps, sea shells, wine, beer bottles, baseball cards, old magazines, antique glass, artwork, books, etc.

3

$\mathcal{L}$earn a sport together: tennis, scuba diving, sailing, skating.

4

*L*earn a foreign language together.

5

*T*ake music lessons together: violin, piano, guitar.

6

*L*earn to dance. Take classes or use a dance video.

7

*T*ake an adult ed class together.

Romance Across the USA

1

*V*isit all 50 states!

*V*isit every national park across the USA. When you're done with that challenge, start on the state parks!

*V*isit towns with romantic names: Love, Arizona; Romance, Arkansas; Loveland, Colorado; Charm, Ohio; Valentine, Texas; Bliss, New York; Romeo, Michigan; Sweet, Idaho; Joy, Illinois.

Romantic Evenings

Romantic Evening #1: "An Evening of Romance"

- ❧ Music: Glenn Miller, George Benson, George Winston, Al Jarreau

- ❧ Movies: Casablanca, Ghost, any Fred Astaire

movie, West Side Story

- Food: French bread & cheese
- Drink: The most expensive champagne you can afford
- Dress: Tuxedos & evening gowns
- Props: Candles, red roses, crystal champagne flutes

Romantic Evening #2: "Beach Party"

- Music: Beach Boys, Monkees
- Movies: *Beach Blanket Bingo*
- Food: Grilled burgers, chips
- Drink: Beer
- Dress: Swimming trunks & bikinis
- Props: Cool sunglasses, sand, beach balls, Coppertone

Romantic Evening #3: "Sex, Sex, Sex!"

- Music: Eurhythmics, *9-1/2 Weeks* soundtrack, Sade
- Movies: *9-1/2 Weeks*, *Body Heat*, *Emmanuel*
- Food: Smoked oysters, Godiva Chocolates
- Drink: Champagne
- Dress: Optional
- Props: According to your particular liking or fetish!

Romantic Evening #4: "1950s Nostalgia"

- Music: Elvis, The Four Freshmen, Buddy Holly
- Movies: Elvis movies, *Picnic*, Doris Day & Rock Hudson movies, *Grease*
- Food: Burgers, onion rings, diner food, Jello
- Drink: Moxie, milk shakes
- Dress: Bobbie sox & saddle shoes, poodle

skirts, Varsity sweaters

❧ Props: A '57 Chevy, horn rimmed glasses.

Romantic Evening #5: "1960s Nostalgia"

❧ Music: Beatles, Rolling Stones, Bob Dylan, Janis Joplin

❧ Movies: *Goldfinger, Yellow Submarine*

❧ Food: Granola

❧ Drink: Electric Kool-Aid

❧ Dress: Hip-hugger jeans, tie-dyed T-shirts, love beads, head bands

❧ Props: Peace signs, happy face pins, Lava Lamps, black light posters

Other romantic themed evenings:

*I*talian: Italian opera; Italian wine; Italian movie, like *La Dolce Vita*.

*H*igh school reunion

- ✎ Music: Top hits from when you were a teenager
- ✎ Movies: Some of your drive-in favorites
- ✎ Food: The junk food of your adolescence
- ✎ Drink: Coca-Cola
- ✎ Dress: Whatever you wore in high school
- ✎ Props: Stuff from that old musty chest in your attic

Mall Dates

1

*H*ead for the nearest mall. Enter the record store. Buy everything ever recorded by Al Jarreau and Luther Vandross. And George Winston. Oh, and George Benson. And don't forget William Ackerman. And, as long as you're there, grab everything by David Lanz, too.

2
. . .

*M*any malls host free concerts, antique shows and other activities.

3
. . .

*W*indow shop and dream together.

4
. . .

*C*reate dates centered on specific stores:

- ❧ The lingerie shop date: Shop for sexy stuff. Go into the dressing room together. Buy an outfit or two. Model them at home. Enjoy!

- ❧ The bookstore date: Browse for books together. Each of you buys two books for the other: One book that you want your partner to read, and one that you know he or she will appreciate. Spend the rest of the evening reading together.

- ❧ The bath shop date: Go shopping for soaps, bubblebath powders, massage oils, etc. Then spend the rest of the evening luxuriating in the tub together.

Wild & Crazy

1

$\mathscr{T}$he theatrically-oriented among you—or the just plain hams—may want to follow one couple's lead and act-out a scene from a favorite movie or play.

This requires both partners to be playful, creative, and flexible. Couples have have played Romeo and Juliet; Harry and Sally (from the movie When Harry Met Sally); and Rick and Ilsa in a variety of scenes from Casablanca.

2

$\mathscr{H}$oward and Janet B. don't act-out movie scenes, but they do sometimes "do crazy things" with costumes at home.

Most of their adventures start with homemade costumes. They rented costumes only once: "My tin-foil creation looked more like a robot from Dr. Who than a Knight In Shining Armor, so I broke down and rented a suit of armor from a local theatre company."

3
. . .

*T*his idea is for couples who like the outdoors, the unusual, and the chance to hit it rich. It's also for very cheap guys looking for engagement rings. You can actually go prospecting for diamonds at Crater of Diamonds State Park in Murfreesboro, Arkansas.

For just $3.50 a day, you can work a furrowed, 35-acre field with shovels, hoes, screens, sifters or your bare hands. Although most hunters find only bits of quartz, calcite, jasper and barite, the mine has yielded tens of thousands of diamonds, with about 20% of them gem quality.

In 1990, one visitor found a four-carat diamond! It was later cut into a flawless gem worth $38,000. The park, actually the crater of an extinct volcano, is located about halfway between Texarkana and Hot Springs. For more info call 501-285-3113.

Turning Chores Into Dates

1
· · ·

If you let your Inner Child out to play, you can make lots of chores into fun times. Adults make raking leaves into work. Children make piles of leaves and leap into them. You and your partner could do the same!

2
· · ·

You can even make cleaning the bathroom romantic, if you're clever enough about it! Here's how one couple does it: 1) They clean the bathroom together, 2) They time themselves to see how quickly they can do it, and 3) They do it in the nude. As you can imagine, they're always bumping into each other, they're hurrying and laughing and making a scene! (And I'll leave it to you to imagine what happens immediately after their chore is done...)

3
. . .

$\mathcal{A}$nd then there's always nude dusting, nude room painting, nude dish washing. (You get the idea.)

Around Town

1
. . .

$\mathcal{T}$he library date.

2
. . .

$\mathcal{T}$he coffee shop date.

3
. . .

$\mathcal{T}$he outdoor concert date.

4
. . .

$\mathcal{T}$he walk in the park date.

5

$\mathcal{A}$ct like a tourist. Call your local Chamber of Commerce and the Convention & Visitors Bureau and get brochures and schedules for all the attractions in your vicinity. Take a tour. Visit the sights.

6

$\mathcal{V}$isit garage sales, flea markets and craft fairs.

7

$\mathcal{V}$isit art museums, planetariums, public gardens.

Random Ideas

1

$\mathcal{G}$et up an hour early. Have breakfast together at a local diner.

2

Stay up late for a midnight snack. Slip out together to a local coffee shop.

3

Go fly a kite.

4

Learn to bake bread. Bake a pie. Make heart-shaped cookies.

5

Roll out the red carpet—literally—for your lover! Find a red rug, maybe rent one. Roll it out your front door and down the stairs. Treat him like royalty. Make her your Queen-for-a-Day!

6

Split a banana split. Dance the night away. Go singing in the rain.

Seasonal Romance

1

$\int$ummer: beaches, walks, summer solstice, surfing, water skiing, rent a convertible

2

$\mathcal{A}$utumn: leaf watching, Christmas/holiday shopping, autumn equinox

3

$\mathcal{W}$inter: ice skating, winter solstice, snowman, sledding, tobogganing, sleigh ride

4

$\int$pring: plant a garden, spring equinox, fly a kite.

Getting to Know You

1

If your life together were a book or a movie, what kind would it be? A comedy? A horror? A thriller? A mystery? A tragedy? A romantic comedy? A foreign film? A grade-B movie? An X-rated movie? An Academy Award winner? A treasured classic? Fiction or non-fiction?

What roles are each of you playing? Which roles might you like to try on? Hero? Heroine? Good guy? Bad guy? Martyr? Jester? The strong, silent type? The silently-suffering type? The temptress? The Prince? The Princess? The Wicked Witch? The breadwinner? The mother? The bumbling idiot? The jokester? The handyman? The lover?

2

Get the book *Illusions,* by Richard Bach. Read pages 101 to 113.

3

$\mathcal{T}$ake turns asking each other questions from the book *Romantic Questions*.

Stretch Your Limits

1

$\mathcal{R}$ead aloud to each other.

2

$\mathcal{H}$ave your astrological charts analyzed. Call professional astrologer Eric Linter in Boston at 617-524-5275.

Sexy Dates

1

$\mathcal{S}$pend an evening searching for her G-spot. (You may not find it, but you'll both have fun trying!)

2
. . .

*A*phrodisiac dates! Experiment with some alleged aphrodisiacs. Couldn't hurt. Might help! Oysters, caviar, nutmeg, saffron, ginger, fenugreek, mushrooms, chocolate!

3
. . .

*M*ake an appointment to make love. Hey, sometimes you just gotta schedule these things in! Mark it in her Day-Timer; schedule it in his computer; reserve a time on your wall calendar.

4
. . .

*L*ock the doors, draw the curtains, send the kids away. Then dine in the nude. Or merely scantily clad. (Don't forget to schedule enough time for "dessert.")

Games People Play

1
. . .

*W*hen's the last time the two of you played Monopoly, chess, Scrabble or cards together?

2
. . .

*D*o the Sunday crossword puzzle together.

3
. . .

*G*o bowling. Shoot pool. Play croquet.

Fun, Fun, Fun!

1
. . .

*D*o the country western "thing." Learn to Two-Step. Learn some country line dances. Dress the part: Get some cowboy boots and hats.

Create a romantic environment with candles. Place dozens of candles throughout your home: in the dining room, living room, up the stairs, in the bathroom, in the bedroom. If this doesn't inspire an evening of romance, nothing will!

ABCs of Love

"Do you know your ABCs?" Ask your partner to pick a letter. Then read the list of corresponding words. He or she has 24 hours in which to get a romantic gift or perform a romantic gesture based on any one of the key words.

A is for Attitude, Available, Accept, Ardor, Accolades, Admire, Aphrodisiacs, A' La Mode, Anniversary, Ambrosia, Ardent, Athens, Australia

B is for Boudoir, B&B, B&Bs, Buttercups, Beaches, Blue, Books, Boston, Bings, Balloons,

Bicycling, Broadway, Brandy, Bubblebaths, Bahamas

C is for Champagne, Creativity, Candlelight, Cunnilingus, Candy, Chocolate, Convertibles, Casablanca, Cognac, Caviar, Chivalry, Crabtree & Evelyn

D is for Diamonds, Dinner, Daffodils, Dancing, Dating, Dolls, Dirty Dancing

E is for Enthusiasm, Energy, Excitement, Emeralds, Earrings, Elvis, Erotic, Exotic, Expensive, Escapes

F is for Flirting, Fantasies, Feminine, Faithful, Fellatio, France, Flowers, Fruits, Frenching, Foreplay

G is for Garters, Gardenias, Godiva, Getaways, Gifts, Glenn Miller, Gourmet, Greece

H is for Hearts, Humor, Hugs, Hideaways, Horses, Honeymoons, Hawaii, Hershey's Kisses, Hyatt

I is for Intimacy, Intrigue, Italy, Inns, Islands, Ingenuity, Ice Cream, Ice Skating, Interdependent,

Imaginative, Invitation, Incense

J is for Jewelry, Java, Jasmine, Jello, Jazz, Journey, Joyful, Jacuzzi

K is for Kissing, Kinky, Kittens, Koala Bears

L is for Love, Lingerie, Laughing, Love Letters, Lilacs, Lace, Leather, Leo Buscaglia, Lobsters, Lovemaking, Limousines, Love songs, London

M is for Monogamy, Marriage, Masculine, M&M's, Massage, Movies, Mistletoe, Music, Mozart

N is for Negligee, Naughty, Nibble, Nighttime, Nubile, Novelty, Nurture, Nymph, Naples, Nightcap, Nape, Nepal, Necklace

O is for Orgasm, Opera, Orchid, Outrageous, Outdoors

P is for Passion, Perfume, Poppies, Poetry, Persimmons, Paris, Polkas, Panties, Pizza, Photos, Pearls, Picnics, Playfulness, Purple

Q is for Quiet, Quaint, Quality, Queen, Quebec, Question, QE2, Quiche, Quiver

R is for Rendezvous, Roses, Rubies, Red, Reading, Rome, Rituals, Riviera, Restful, Rapture, Rings, Rio, Rainbows

S is for Sex

T is for Talking, Teasing, Tulips, Titillating, Theatre, Togetherness, Tickets, Toasts, Toys, Trains, Trinidad

U is for Umbrellas, Uxorious, Undress, Undulate, Urges, Unexpected, Union, Under the Spreading Chestnut Tree

V is for Violets, Virgins, Vibrators, Venice, Venus, Valentines, Vegetables, Victoria's Secret

W is for Wine, Wisteria, Walking Hand-In-Hand, Weddings

X is for X-Rated, Xerographic, Xylophones, Xmas

Y is for Yachts, Yes, Yellow, Yin & Yang, Young-at-heart

Z is for Zany, Zanzibar, Zeal, Zings, Zodiac, Zurich

Why Be Romantic??

1

*W*hy be romantic? Because romance is the expression of love. It's the action step of love. You see, without romance, love is merely a concept, an ideal, a nice idea. Romance is what brings love alive in the world.

2

*W*hy be romantic? So you will enjoy life more. Yes, you. Your partner will benefit too—but one of the secrets of true romantics is that we know that our own lives are more fun, joyful and passionate when we express our feelings of love.

Motivating Your Partner

$\mathscr{A}$ major reason why some people aren't romantic is that a lack of it doesn't affect them. If you want him (or her) to be more romantic, but he's satisfied with the status quo…"Well, tough luck—that's your problem!" he says/thinks. The solution? Simple: Make it his problem. I've observed that people tend to solve problems that they define as problems that relate personally to themselves.

How do you "make it his problem"? Well, you start by telling him up-front what you want (more romance), and how you want it (circle your favorite items in this book!).

Tell him what action you're going to take if he doesn't meet you half-way. Then select activities that you know will strike home with him: Withhold sex. Stop cooking dinner. Stop helping him with selected chores. Stop being romantic toward him.

He'll either get the message or leave. Either way, you win.

2
. . .

*P*ositive reinforcement works—negative reinforcement doesn't. Study after study confirms this, and yet most of us ignore it! Here's the simple rule:

Reward behavior that you want repeated.

That's it! If you want her to be more romantic, lavish attention on her every time she's the least bit considerate or loving. DO NOT punish her for not being romantic: Nagging doesn't work! You see, positive reinforcement is sometimes a longer, slower process—but its effects are more long-term.

Negative reinforcement, on the other hand, usually works immediately, but resentment soon builds-up, and the effects don't last long-term.

Romantic Homework

1
· · ·

*A*re you ready for some homework? Each of you titles a page "Things I Want You to Do for Me & With Me." The goal here is to create as long a list as possible—at least 25 items long.

The lists can cover anything and everything! Now, trade lists. Talk about them. What's realistic? What's unrealistic? How important are certain items? Now, take back your own list and prioritize the top 20 items. (This may take a while!)

Then, trade lists again. Cross-out the five items you care least about. Take your own list back. You cross-out five more items—the things you want to do least. You each now have a list of 10 things that you want from your partner, and that your partner is likely to act-on.

2
· · ·

*C*reate four lists: a "Wish List"—for things you

want; a "Fantasy List"—for sensual and sexual activities you desire; a "Couple's To-Do List"—for activities/restaurants/movies; and a "Dream List"—for travel and vacations.

3
. . .

*T*urn romance into a habit—a good habit. It may feel awkward, unnatural or contrived at first, but keep at it!

Research has shown that it takes about three weeks to form new habits. If you repeat an activity or thought pattern several times a day over three weeks, you'll get it ingrained into that stubborn brain of yours! Go for it!

For Men Only

1
. . .

*M*any men view romance as "giving in" to a woman. It makes perfect sense to me that you'd resist being romantic if you see it that way.

It's natural for people to resist what they view as coercion. Here's a suggestion: Don't give-in. Don't do what she expects. Don't do what society expects. Don't try to live-up to some fairy tale of what the perfect man should be. Don't follow some soap opera stereotype of a great guy.

Here's what you could do instead: Express your own feelings in your own way. That's all there is to it. It is possible to retain your individuality, express your own feelings, do it your own way, and please her—all at the same time!

2
. . .

*R*omance is like exercising: You know it's good for you, but its difficult—sometimes actually painful!—at first.

But, as any coach will tell you, the benefits will keep building if you'll just keep up the effort. And after a while, this "chore" will become a habit, and you'll be healthier and happier.

A lot of guys who are He-Men in the Muscle Department, and Supermen in the Boardroom, are 90-Pound Weaklings when in comes to intimacy and love. C'mon, guys, don't let the women kick sand in your face!

3

*P*lan a date for Superbowl Sunday! (After she wakes up from fainting she'll be delighted!) Tape the game on your VCR so you can watch it later, of course.

For Women Only

1

*P*sst! Ladies! Here's the worst-kept secret in the world: Guys do want and need romance. I don't know why we play this game around it, but most men do.

Frankly, many men are quite sentimental. And

every tough guy has a soft spot. Look for it—you'll
find it.

2
. . .

*H*ard to motivate your guy? Is he a sports nut?
Great! Do something he'll understand: Put him on
a "Point System"—Turn romance into a "game."

Write your own rules, post them on the refrigerator
door, create score sheets, and keep statistics.
Award him points for various romantic activities.

When he racks-up 100 points, he wins something
that truly motivates him—You decide what:
Anything from sex to pizza, or from backrubs to
doing his most hated chore for him!

3
. . .

*S*ome inspiration for "erotic dates" can be found
in the pages of various masterpieces of "erotica for
women":

- *Slow Hand: Women Writing Erotica*, edited by
  Michele Slung

- *Fever: Sensual Stories by Women Writers*, another collection from M. Slung

- *Women On Top*, by Nancy Friday

- *Good Sex: Stories From Real People*, by Julia Hutton

- *Gates of Paradise*, by Alberto Manguel

- *Erotica,* edited by Margaret Reynolds

- *The Doctor Is In*, by Charlotte Rose

Extra Items

1

*O*ne way to generate romantic ideas is to "break the pattern" of your daily lives. Changing any one thing, or a combination of them, has the potential for creating new and exciting opportunities in your lives.

What are your patterns? What time do you wake up in the morning? What do you eat for breakfast?

Where do you eat? How do you dress? How long
do you work? Where do you drive? What do you do
with the kids? What do you watch on TV? How
often do you talk by phone with each other?

Erotic Dates

1
. . .

*W*hat kind of fun could you have with Chocolate
Body Paints?? A handy set of "His & Hers" 8 oz.
jars are available from The Celebration Fantastic
Catalog. Call 800-CELEBRATE.

2
. . .

*F*orget "strip poker"—try playing "strip dinner"!
With each course you each remove one article of
clothing! Make sure you plan plenty of courses!

Mood Music

1

For creating a mellow mood, albums by Nicholas Gunn:

- *The Sacred Fire*
- *The Music of the Grand Canyon*

2

For creating an erotic mood, two albums by Enigma:

- *MCMXC A.D.*
- *The Cross of Change*

3

For creating a thoughtful mood, albums by George Winston:

- *Summer*

❧ *Autumn*

❧ *Winter Into Spring*

4

$\mathscr{M}$usic for creating an uplifting mood, by Eric Tingstad and Nancy Rumbel:

❧ *Homeland*

❧ *Give and Take*

❧ *In the Garden*

5

$\mathscr{M}$usic for creating a mystical mood, by Andreas Vollenweider:

❧ *White Winds*

❧ *Down to the Moon*

6

$\mathscr{T}$he world's most romantic piano concertos (take my word for it):

- *Mozart's Piano Concerto No. 21 in C*
- *Beethoven's Piano Concerto No. 5 in E flat*
- *Schumann's Concerto in A Minor for Piano & Orchestra*
- *Grieg's Concerto in A Minor for Piano & Orchestra*

Fun, Fun, Fun!

1

This one could keep the two of you busy for weeks! Have a custom jigsaw puzzle created for the two of you, based on your design, artwork or photo.

2

What's your favorite card game? Spend an evening playing poker or gin rummy, kings or cribbage. Place some bets to make it more interesting.

3

*P*lay strip poker together! For the more intellectual among you, play strip chess!

4

*B*e conventional—attend a convention together. Fanatics love to gather! Science fiction fanatics, Star Trekkers, comic book collectors, quilt makers, car buffs, RVers, Beatles fans, guys named Bob, romance novel writers, etc.

Kinda Crazy

1

*S*erenade her! Sing her favorite love song, or "Your Song," to her. Get a friend to accompany you on guitar.

2

$\mathscr{I}$f your partner is a beer lover to rival Norm Peterson...plan a date to "Beer Camp"! Believe it or not, The American Museum of Brewing History and Arts, in Fort Mitchell, Kentucky, runs a three-day Beer Camp! Call 606-341-7223.

3

$\mathscr{F}$or creating a romantic atmosphere everywhere you go, keep candles in your car at all times. Bring them into McDonald's when you stop for a burger! (Why should you care if other people thing you're strange?!?)

Use Your Creativity

1

$\mathscr{R}$omantic Challenge #1: Create a date that is classic and conservative, but thoughtful in the extreme.

2

*R*omantic Challenge #2: Create a date that is sexy to the point of nearly being illegal.

3

*R*omantic Challenge #3: Create a date that is not necessarily wild, but is totally unexpected from a person of your personality style.

Going Places!

1

*F*eeling adventurous? Pack two bags, call your travel agent, and ask for any discount tickets for vacation packages leaving anytime in the next 24 hours. Regardless of what the destination is—go!

2

*I*s your honey a Wizard of Oz fanatic? If so, take him or her to the Judy Garland Museum! Rare photos, rare recordings and memorabilia. The Yellow Brick Road is in Grand Rapids, Minnesota. Call 218-326-6431.

3
. . .

$\mathcal{T}$ry an "ultra all-inclusive luxury resort for couples only" at one of Sandals Resorts on Jamaica, Antigua, St. Lucia or Barbados. Call 800-SAN-DALS.

4
. . .

$\mathcal{A}$nd here are some specific Bed and Breakfast resource books for you:

- *Bed & Breakfasts and Country Inns—Inspected, Rated and Approved*, by the American Bed & Breakfast Association
- *Bed and Breakfast U.S.A.*, by Betty Rundback
- *Recommended Romantic Inns*, from the authors of the Recommended Country Inns Series

5

*I*f money is no object, you may want to take your honey on a three-week round-the-world trip on the Concorde! Only $52,000 per person! Call INTRAV at 800-456-8100.

6

*V*isit the real bridges of Madison County—in Winterset, Iowa!

Togetherness

1

*B*ake Christmas cookies together. Let your creativity run wild while decorating them.

2

*D*esign your own holiday cards. You don't have to be Picasso to be creative!

$\mathcal{D}$esign a whole line of greeting cards from the two of you. Create a recognizable style that all your friends and family will recognize as they receive custom birthday cards, anniversary cards, holiday cards, Halloween cards, etc., from the two of you.

Poetic Dates

1

$\mathcal{H}$e plays Romeo, she plays Juliet. Read aloud to each other.

2

$\mathcal{P}$ick a passage from your Favorite Book of All Time. Read it aloud to your partner. Share with him or her its significance in your life.

$\mathcal{P}$ick a steamy passage from an erotic book to read aloud to each other in bed. Some modest suggestions:

- *Little Birds*, by Anais Nin
- *Lady Chatterley's Lover*, by D.H. Lawrence
- *Tropic of Cancer*, by Henry Miller
- *Yellow Silk*, edited by Lily Pond & Richard Russo

4

$\mathcal{F}$ind a copy of Elizabeth Barrett Browning's poem How Do I Love Thee? (Let me count the ways...) Spend an evening rewriting the poem to list the many ways you love each other.

Rendezvous

1

$\mathscr{M}$eet for drinks after work.

2

$\mathscr{M}$eet for lunch during a busy week.

3

$\mathscr{M}$eet at a local motel for a little "afternoon delight."

4

$\mathscr{M}$eet for dinner at the airport. Dream about far-away places.

5

$\mathscr{M}$eet at work for an in-office picnic.

Up, Up and Away!

1

*G*o for a romantic ride in a hot air balloon.

2

*H*ave you ever considered taking flying lessons together?

3

*F*or the truly courageous, try sky diving!

4

*F*or the extremely courageous, try hang gliding!

5

*F*or the slightly courageous, try bungee jumping!

Out and About

1

*B*efore you can sail off into the sunset together, it might be helpful to take sailing lessons together.

2

*T*hey tell me that surfing is a blast.

3

*H*ow about scuba diving?

4

*H*ow about an afternoon of snorkeling?

5

*H*ow about a day of just sitting on the beach, reading, talking and sipping daiquiris?

6

*W*hile on the beach, challenge each other to a sandcastle building contest. The loser has to run to the ice cream stand for snacks.

Role Playing

1

*W*hile out to dinner, take on the roles of characters from your favorite movie. How would Indiana Jones be enjoying dinner? What would Princess Leia talk about this evening?

2

*S*pend and evening out pretending that you're characters from your favorite movie, TV show or book. James Bond? Scarlett O'Hara? Captain James T. Kirk? Lucille Ball?

3

Each of you choose a favorite character from the movies, Broadway or literature, and act-out meeting one another, falling in love and seducing one another. (Could be fun for an evening—could go on for weeks!)

4

Pretend you're tourists visiting your own town. Visit places you've never gotten around to before. See things through new eyes.

5

Pretend you're vacationing foreigners who don't speak any English. Have fun asking directions and ordering in restaurants while pretending to not understand English.

Party On!

1

*T*hrow a surprise birthday party for your partner.

2

*T*hrow a surprise party for no specific reason.

3

*G*uys: Get together with several of your buddies and throw a surprise "Wife/Girlfriend Appreciation Party." The highlight of the party is when you toast the gals with champagne: Each of you, one at a time, stands up and recites a romantic, prewritten toast to your honey.

4

*G*als: Get together with some of your girlfriends and plan a surprise "Husband/Boyfriend Appreciation Party." Serve their favorite beer;

maybe watch a football game on TV; maybe get together and write a song about all of them—then sing it to them!

5

$\mathscr{H}$ost a wine tasting party.

6

$\mathscr{H}$ost a "Taste Test" party, in which you hold blind taste testings to see of your friends can identify these foods:

- Coke vs. Pepsi vs. Diet Coke vs. Diet Pepsi, etc.
- Budweiser vs. Heineken vs. Coors vs. Miller, etc.
- Different peanut butter brands
- Different potato chip brands
- Different types of breakfast cereal

Acting Up

1
· · ·

*H*ire a limousine for the evening. Make reservations at the best restaurant in town. Dress in tuxedo and evening gown. Hire a photographer to snap your picture as you arrive at the restaurant. Pretend you're famous—watch people gawk and try to figure out who you are!

2
· · ·

*J*oin a local community theatre group. Whether you're playing the lead, singing in the chorus or designing scenery, you'll have a blast!

3
· · ·

*A*ct-out your favorite erotic fantasy together.

4
. . .

*C*hoose fantasy roles—and stay in character for an entire day!

Calming Down

1
. . .

*L*earn to meditate together. Buy a book or take a class together to get you started.

2
. . .

*T*ake a weekend to calm down...attend a religious, spiritual or meditational retreat.

3
. . .

*T*ake a different kind of vacation...one designed to deepen your spirit and expand your mind. Check out a great book called *Vacations That Can Change Your Life: Adventures, Retreats & Workshops for the Mind, Body & Spirit*, by Ellen Lederman.

4

Make a cassette tape of romantic, instrumental music. Go for a drive in the country while listening to the soothing sounds. Don't speak a word

Getting Out

1

Run a race together. Maybe a local "Fun Run." Maybe a fundraiser for a local charity.

2

Get serious about it: Run some 10-K races.

3

Get really serious about it: Train for running a marathon.

4
. . .

$\mathcal{G}$rab your backpacks and go for a day hike.

Marathons

1
. . .

$\mathcal{C}$atch a movie marathon at a local theatre.

2
. . .

$\mathcal{C}$reate your own movie marathon by renting a bunch of movies that form a theme.

3
. . .

$\mathcal{C}$reate a TV show marathon. Videotape a bunch of your favorite TV shows over several months. Save them up for a 24-hour TV marathon.

4
. . .

$\mathcal{S}$pend a night of non-stop, marathon lovemaking!

Picture This

1
. . .

*B*uy a bunch of cheap, throw-away cameras. Spend a Saturday afternoon on a "Photo Safari."

2
. . .

*B*uy an expensive camera, take photography classes together, and get serious about it.

3
. . .

*T*ake turns shooting portrait shots of each other. Try to capture the true essence of each other's personality.

4
. . .

*F*or the truly adventurous, spend an evening posing for elegant, erotic photos of each other.

Group Activities

1
. . .

$\mathcal{J}$oin a local Marriage Encounter group. You'll deepen your relationship with like-minded couples.

2
. . .

$\mathcal{J}$oin a local political campaign.

3
. . .

$\mathcal{T}$ake horseback riding lessons together.

4
. . .

$\mathcal{P}$lay "Twister" with a group of friends.

Something Old

1

Attend a program sponsored by your local Historical Society.

2

Spend the day with your grandparents or great-grandparents. Share stories about your family history.

3

Go on a tour of old homes in your area.

4

Grab your high school yearbooks and spend an evening sharing memories.

Something New

1
. . .

Learn to play a video game. (You may need to hire a local youngster to teach you.)

2
. . .

Whether or not you're interested in buying a new house, attend some local Open Houses. Discuss your ideas of the "Perfect Home."

3
. . .

Visit new restaurants in your area. Don't go to the same old places on every date!

4
. . .

Catch a new act at a local comedy club.

Friends

1

*G*ather a group of friends and plan "Progressive Dinners" once a month.

2

*G*ather a group of friends, all of whom have small children, and take turns hosting "Group Pajama Parties." You take turns hosting all the kids overnight, so all the other couples can have more time alone.

3

*T*hrow a massive Superbowl party. Attendees must dress as football players, cheerleaders, referees or crazy fans!

4

*H*ost a "Murder Mystery" party. Who-done-it??

Roll the Dice

1

*H*ead to Las Vegas for the weekend. (Or to Atlantic City!)

2

*G*amble on a Mississippi River Boat!

3

*P*lay a complete, non-stop game of Monopoly.

4

*L*ist twelve different sexual activities on a sheet of paper. Roll two dice to determine which activity the two of you will share tonight! (She rolls the dice this time—he rolls the dice the next time.) Nobody loses!

Questions & Answers

1

$\mathscr{D}$o you celebrate one another at any time other than your anniversary? Celebrate your anniversary every month.

2

$\mathscr{H}$ow did you meet? Where did you meet? Visit that place. Re-enact your meeting. Take some artistic license to make your"second meeting" memorably romantic!

3

$\mathscr{D}$o you rush through meals, or do you savor them together? Make time. Create your own personal rituals around meals.

4

*W*hen's the last time you watched a sunset together? A sunrise? All it takes is a little desire, a little time and a little planning.

Asking for a Date

1

*S*end him an e-mail invitation to a date.

2

*A*ttach a note to a single red rose. The note includes one line from a romantic song, along with your request for a date.

3

*B*uy two tickets to something (a show, a sporting event, a concert) and mail them to your partner, along with a note asking him or her for a date.

4

. . .

*F*ax your request for a date! (Make sure it doesn't get intercepted by an office colleague!)

5

. . .

*W*rite a short poem that describes the date you're proposing.

Theme Dates II

Romantic Evening #1: "Erotic Romance"

*S*et a sexy mood with music by Sade or Enigma; light the scene with candles; serve champagne and a tray of aphrodisiacs; dress in your sexiest outfit; remove all distractions; draw the curtains…and prepare to spend an entire evening of sexual exploration.

Romantic Evening #2: "1950s Nostalgia"

*S*pin those old 45s by Elvis, The Four Freshmen

and Buddy Holly. Dress in bobbie socks, saddle shoes, poodle skirt; or varsity sweater. Serve burgers and moxie. And take your honey for a romantic ride in a '57 Chevy!

Romantic Evening #3: "1960s Nostalgia"

*D*ress is hip-hugger jeans, tie-dyed T-shirts, love bead and head bands. Blast music by the Beatles, Rolling Stones, Bob Dylan and Janis Joplin. Make love by the light of your Lava Lamp.

Romantic Evening #4: "High School Nostalgia"

*G*ather music from when you were a teenager; rent some movies that were big during those years; dig out your high school year books...and create a custom date based on your own history.

Romantic Evening #5: "Viva Italiana!"

*G*ather all things Italian: Wines, foods, opera,

posters and movies. Create an evening of romance based on those hot-blooded Mediterraneans!

More Romantic Evenings

$\int$ ome modest suggestions to spark your imagination:

- ✷ Romantic Evening #6: "New York, New York"
- ✷ Romantic Evening #7: "Lingerie Fashion Show"
- ✷ Romantic Evening #8: "Gourmet Delight"
- ✷ Romantic Evening #9: "The Bridges of Madison County"

You Can Quote Me On That!

1

$\mathcal{C}$reate a romantic date based on the following quote:

*"I do love nothing in the world so well as you;
is not that strange?"*

~ William Shakespeare

Copy this quote onto a card, give it to your partner,
and plan to do something really strange. (Defining
exactly what constitutes "strange" is up to you!)

2

*C*reate a date based on this romantic quote:

*"My most brilliant achievement was my ability
to be able to persuade my wife to marry me."*

~ Winston Churchill

Plan a date—an outrageous, stupendously
wonderful date—that will become your most
brilliant achievement.

3

*C*reate a romantic date based on this quote:

"Love is, above all, the gift of oneself."

~ Jean Anouilh

Copy this quote onto a card, give it to your partner, and create a date in which you give yourself to your partner.

4
. . .

*C*reate a romantic date based on this quote:

> *"A love song is just a caress set to music."*
>
> ~ Sigmund Romberg

Copy this quote onto a card, give it to your partner and spend an evening combining the two concepts of love songs and caresses!

5
. . .

*C*reate a romantic date based on this quote:

> *"The heart that loves is always young."*
>
> ~ Greek proverb

Copy this quote onto a card, give it to your partner, and do something that proves you're still young: go to a playground; go on a picnic; go for a stroll.

6
. . .

$\mathcal{C}$reate a date based on this romantic quote:

"The madness of love is the greatest of heaven's blessings."

~ *Plato*

Copy this quote onto a card, give it to your partner and plan something "mad" like taking a surprise day off work.

7
. . .

$\mathcal{C}$reate a date based on an inspirational quote:

"God is love, and love is joy. All the universe has come from love and unto love all things return."

~ *Juan Mascaro*

Copy this quote onto a card, give it to your partner and plan a joyful date that reconnects you with your spiritual beliefs.

8

Create a date based on this quote:

"Love, you know, seeks to make happy rather than to be happy."

~ *Ralph Connor*

Copy this quote onto a card, give it to your partner and plan a date that is specifically designed to touch his or her heart.

9
· · ·

Create a date based on a quote:

"Love is a little haven of refuge from the world."

~ *Bertrand Russell*

Copy this quote onto a card, give it to your partner and create your very own haven of refuge in your home. Maybe you'll have to escape to a bed and breakfast in order to find a safe haven.

10

*C*reate a date based on a quote: Be on the lookout for quotes that can inspire date ideas. You're surrounded by great quotes all the time—in newspapers, magazines, books, TV and radio.

Song-Inspired Dates

1

*C*reate a date based on the song:

"EIGHT DAYS A WEEK"
BY THE BEATLES

Give your partner a copy of this song, and find a way to squeeze and "extra" day out of a week sometime next month.

2
  . . .

$\mathcal{C}$reate a date based on the song:

"CHATTANOOGA CHOO-CHOO"
BY GLENN MILLER

Give your partner a copy of this song, and get two tickets for a train ride—maybe a dinner train.

3
  . . .

$\mathcal{C}$reate a date based on the song:

"LIGHT MY FIRE"
BY THE DOORS

Give your partner a copy of this song, build a fire in the fireplace and light your lover's fire!

4
  . . .

$\mathcal{C}$reate a date based on a song:

"YOU ARE THE SUNSHINE OF MY LIFE"
BY STEVIE WONDER

Give your partner a copy of this song, and spend a

day out in the sun! Hit a beach, dine outdoors, drive a convertible!

Book a Date!

1
. . .

*C*reate a date based on the book:

LOVE SIGNS
BY LINDA GOODMAN

Give your partner a copy of this book; it details the pros and cons of every match-up of two Zodiac signs. Spend an evening analyzing your relationship!

2
. . .

*C*reate a date based on the book:

THE JOY OF SEX
BY ALEX COMFORT

Give your partner a copy of this book. Pick a page. Follow the recipe!

3

Create a date based on the book:

OFF THE BEATEN PATH—A GUIDE TO MORE THAN 1,000 SCENIC AND INTERESTING PLACES STILL UNCROWDED AND INVITING

Give your partner a copy of this book. Find someplace nearby and head there ASAP.

4

Create a date based on the book:

THE ART OF KISSING
BY WILLIAM CANE

Give your partner a copy of this book. Spend an evening exploring different kissing techniques!

5

Create a date based on the book:

A WHACK ON THE SIDE OF THE HEAD: HOW YOU CAN BE MORE CREATIVE
BY ROGER VONOECH

Get a copy of this book, and spend an evening brainstorming ideas for dates with your partner.

TV Times

1
· · ·
Create a date based on the TV show:

Home Improvement

Catch a couple episodes together. Spend an evening tuning-up your car. Reorganize your tools. Build something.

2
· · ·
Create a date based on a TV show:

Star Trek: The Next Generation

Catch a couple episodes together. If you had access to a real "Holo-Deck," what kind of adventures would you program into the computer? How could you enact some of these adventures in real life?

3

Create a date based on the TV show:

Seinfeld

Watch several episodes together. Spend the day in Manhattan; hang-out in a diner; do "nothing."

Movie-Inspired Dates

1

Create a date based on the movie:

Dirty Dancing

Watch the movie together, then create your own, custom "Dirty Dance"...and dance your way into bed!

2

Create a date based on the movie:

Love Story

Watch the movie together. Discuss what the two of you would do if one of you had only weeks to live. What would you change about your lives in order to cherish each other more?!

3
. . .

Create a date based on the movie:

Somewhere in Time

Watch the movie together. Imagine the two of you meeting in a different era. Talk about your favorite time period. Rent costumes from that time— fantasize!

4
. . .

Create a date based on the movie:

From Here to Eternity

Watch the movie together. Head for the nearest beach...you'll know what to do!

Mission Impossible

1
. . .

Do the impossible: Get him Superbowl tickets!

2
. . .

Do the impossible: Meet her at the airport when she knows you're tied-up and can't make it. Devote the entire evening to her.

3
. . .

Do the impossible: Get tickets to a sold-out show.

Full of Hot Air!

1
. . .

Visit one of America's many hot air balloon festivals:

- The U.S. National Hot Air Balloon Festival: early August, in Indianola, Iowa. Call 515-961-8415.

- The "Greit Oktoberfest Balloon Rally": late August/early September, in Dansville, New York. Call 716-335-3708.

- The International Balloon Fiesta: mid-October, in Albuquerque, New Mexico. Call 800-284-2282.

For a free one-year subscription to Greg Godek's *LoveLetter Newsletter* send your name and address to:

LoveLetter
Sourcebooks
P.O. Box 372
Naperville, IL 60566

Would you like to see your name in print in a future book?! If you have a romantic, creative or outrageous story that you would like to share, please send it to:

Love Stories
Sourcebooks
P.O. Box 372
Naperville, IL 60566

Would you be interested in having Greg Godek present a speech or seminar to your group? For more information, please call his office at:

630-961-3900

Other books in this series include:

Romantic Fantasies: & Other Sexy Ways of Expressing Your Love
ISBN: 1-57071-154-2; $6.95

Romantic Mischief: The Playful Side of Love
ISBN: 1-57071-151-8; $6.95

Romantic Questions: Growing Closer Through
Intimate Conversation
ISBN: 1-57071-152-6; $6.95

Also by Gregory J.P. Godek

1001 Ways to Be Romantic
5th Anniversary Edition of the Bestselling Classic!
ISBN: 1-883518-05-9; $14.95

1001 More Ways to Be Romantic
ISBN: 0-9629803-2-3; $11.95

To order these books or any other of our many publications, please contact your local bookseller, gift store or call Sourcebooks. Books by Gregory J.P. Godek are available in book and gift stores across North America. Get a copy of our catalog by writing or faxing:

Sourcebooks
P. O. Box 372
Naperville, IL 60566
(630) 961-3900
FAX: (630) 961-2168